when the earth was young

other books by david yeadon

Exploring Small Towns Vol. 1—Southern California

Exploring Small Towns Vol. 2—Northern California

Hidden Restaurants of Southern California

Hidden Restaurants of Northern California

Sumptuous Indulgence on a Shoestring—a Cookbook

Wine Tasting in California

The New York Book of Bars, Pubs and Taverns

Hidden Corners of New England

Hidden Corners of the Mid-Atlantic States

Nooks and Crannies of New York City

Back Road Journeys in America Vol. 1—West Coast

when the earth was young

songs of the american indian

DAVID YEADON

DOUBLEDAY & COMPANY, INC., GARDEN CITY, NEW YORK

1978

For my Mother and Father

The poems in this collection are taken from the Bureau of American Ethnology bulletins, and are in the public domain. All other material in this book is copyrighted.

Library of Congress Cataloging in Publication Data

Yeadon, David.
   When the earth was young.

   1. Indian poetry—North America—Translations into English.   2. English poetry—Translations from Indian languages.   I. Title.
PM198.E3Y4   897
ISBN 0-385-12466-x
Library of Congress Catalog Card Number 76–42430

contents

acknowledgments

Permission has been granted for publication of songs and chants from the following sources:

page 87   *The Fighting Cheyenne,* George Bird Grinnell. Charles Scribner's Sons, New York, 1915.

pages 16, 21, 72 and 111   *The Indian's Book: Songs and Legends of the American Indians,* Natalie Curtis. Dover Publications, Inc., New York, 1968. Reprinted through the permission of the publisher.

pages 44 and 47   *Navajo Legends,* Washington Matthews. Houghton Mifflin Company, Boston, 1897.

page 67   *Navajo Myths, Prayers and Songs* with texts and translations by Washington Matthews, edited by Pliny Earle Goddard. University of California Press, Publications in American Archaeology and Ethnology, Vol. 5, No. 2. Published in 1907 by the Regents of the University of California, reprinted by permission of the University of California Press.

pages 6, 11, 31 and 39   *Singing for Power: Song Magic of the Papago Indians of Southern Arizona,* Ruth Murray Underhill, Copyright © 1966 by Ruth Murray Underhill. Reprinted by permission of the University of California Press.

The author is also most grateful to librarians at the New York Public Library and the Smithsonian Institute Library in Washington, D.C., for their assistance in locating valuable source material.

songs of the american indian

The words and thoughts contained in this book are some of the most beautiful in American literature. They express the soul and spirit of cultures, now destroyed and lost. They reflect an understanding of the unity of all life—of a world in which man exists in harmony with all living things and is part of a natural rhythm which shapes his environment and his whole existence.

To the American Indian, such understanding was intuitive. These songs and chants express concepts which were as obvious and natural to him as electricity is to our present-day society. They were not contrived for idle entertainment, neither were they sung for the benefit of a few discerning listeners; they were part of the tribal fabric, full of meaning and power—direct communications with the infinite.

There is much we can learn—or relearn—from the simple words of these songs.

David Yeadon

earth

When a Horse Neighs

Daybreak appears
When a horse neighs.

There I Will See the Dawn

A low range of mountains, toward them I am running.
From the top of these mountains I will see the dawn.

The Morning Star

The morning star is up.
I cross the mountains into the light of the sea.

Come All!

Come all! Stand up!
Just over there the dawn is coming.
Now I hear
Soft laughter.

There!

There!
There!
Beautiful white-rising has dawned.
Beautiful yellow-rising has dawned.
There!
There!

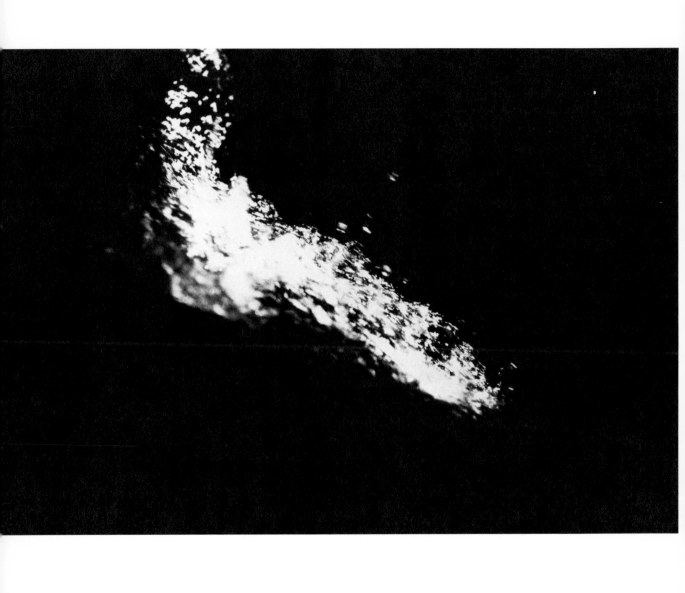

Day Is Here!

Day is here! Day is here, is here!
Arise, my son, lift your eyes.
Day is here! Day is here, is here!
Look up, my son, and see the day.
Day is here! Day is here, is here!

Song to Bring Fair Weather

You, whose day it is, make it beautiful.
Get out your rainbow colors,
So it will be beautiful.

The Eagle's Song

The sun's rays
Lie along my wings
And stretch beyond their tips.

Mountain Side

Mountain side, mountain side,
With the drizzling light brown dust storm,
Mountain side, mountain side.
Over there
Under the light of dawn,
When the morning wind comes,
With that flower wind blowing,
Mountain side, mountain side.

Mountain side, mountain side,
Light brown slope,
You are moving with the wind.

Over there,
Under the dawn,
When this morning wind comes
It brings with it that flower wind,
O mountain side.
Mountain side,
Light brown slope
Moving with the wind.

The Wind Blows from the Sea

By the sandy water I breathe in the odor of the sea,
From there the wind comes and blows over the world,
By the sandy water I breathe in the odor of the sea,
From there the clouds come and rain falls over the world.

By the sandy water I breathe in the odor of the sea.

Cover My Earth Mother

Cover my earth mother four times with many flowers.
Let the heavens be covered with the banked-up clouds.
Let the earth be covered with fog; cover the earth with rains.
Great waters, rains, cover the earth. Lightning cover the earth.
Let thunder be heard over the earth; let thunder be heard;
Let thunder be heard over the six regions of the earth.

Song of the Rain Chant

Far as man can see,
>   Comes the rain,
>   Comes the rain with me.

From the Rain-Mount,
Rain-Mount far away,
>   Comes the rain,
>   Comes the rain with me.

O'er the corn,
O'er the corn, tall corn,
>   Comes the rain,
>   Comes the rain with me.

'Mid the lightnings,
'Mid the lightnings zigzag,
'Mid the lightnings flashing,
>   Comes the rain,
>   Comes the rain with me.

'Mid the swallows,
'Mid the swallows blue,
Chirping glad together,
        Comes the rain,
        Comes the rain with me.

Through the pollen,
Through the pollen blest,
All in pollen hidden,
        Comes the rain,
        Comes the rain with me.

Far as man can see,
        Comes the rain,
        Comes the rain with me.

Corn Song

The corn grows up.
The waters of the dark clouds drop, drop.
The rain descends.
The waters from the corn leaves drop, drop.
The rain descends.
The waters from the plants drop, drop.
The corn grows up.
The waters of the dark mists drop, drop.

Twelfth Song of the Thunder

The voice that beautifies the land!
The voice above,
The voice of thunder.
Within the dark cloud
Again and again it sounds,
The voice that beautifies the land

The voice that beautifies the land!
The voice below:
The voice of the grasshopper.
Among the plants
Again and again it sounds,
The voice that beautifies the land.

Korosta Katzina Song

Yellow butterflies,
Over the blossoming virgin corn,
With pollen-painted faces
Chase one another in brilliant throng.

Blue butterflies,
Over the blossoming virgin beans,
With pollen-painted faces
Chase one another in brilliant streams.

Over the blossoming corn
Over the virgin corn
Wild bees hum;
Over the blossoming beans
Over the virgin beans
Wild bees hum.

Songs of Life Returning

A slender antelope,
A slender antelope
He is wallowing upon the ground.

The wind stirs the willows.
The wind stirs the grasses.

Fog! Fog!
Lightning! Lightning!
Whirlwind! Whirlwind!

Whirlwind! Whirlwind!
The snowy earth comes gliding, the snowy
        earth comes gliding.

There is dust from the whirlwind,
There is dust from the whirlwind,
The whirlwind on the mountain.

The rocks are ringing,
The rocks are ringing,
They are ringing in the mountains.

The cottonwoods are growing tall,
They are growing tall and verdant.

Butterfly Song

Butterfly, butterfly, butterfly, butterfly,
Oh, look, see it hovering among the flowers,
It is like a baby trying to walk and not knowing how to go
The clouds sprinkle down the rain.

Dream Song

Above the place
Where the minnow maiden sleeps
While her fins move gently in the water,
Flowers droop,
Flowers rise back again.

Song of the Za'Gimag

A bubbling spring
Comes from the hard ground.

Spring Song

As my eyes search the prairie,
I feel the summer in the spring.

The Rock

Unmoved
From time without end,
You rest in the midst of the coming winds,
In the winds
You rest, aged one.
Small grasses grow around you
You are covered with the droppings of birds,
Your top decked with downy feathers.
Oh, aged one.

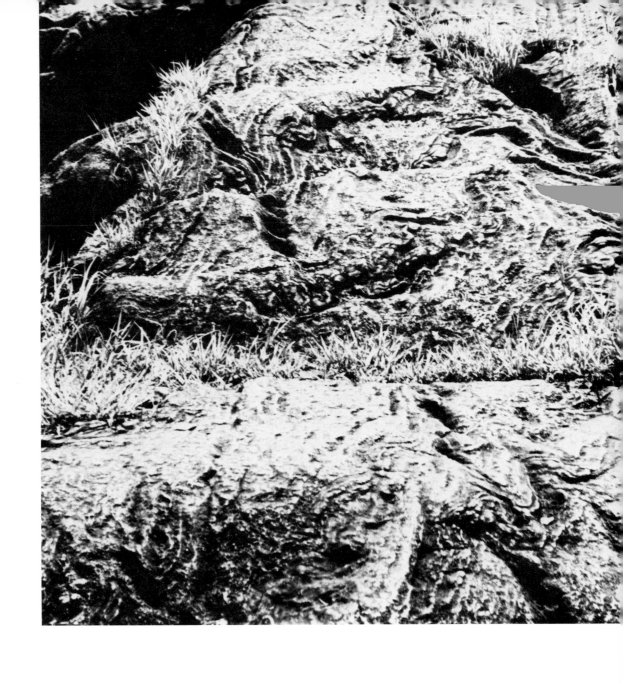

The Water Bug

The water bug is drawing the shadows of evening toward him
across the water.

Blue Evening

Blue evening falls,
Blue evening falls,
Near by, in every direction.
It sets the corn tassels trembling.

The Deer

The deer is taking away the daylight.
The deer is alone in the darkness,
Grazing on a lonely plain,
Near the high mountain.

Brown Owls

Brown owls come here in the blue evening,
They are hooting about,
They are shaking their wings and hooting.

The Sunset

The sun is slowly departing,
It is slower in its setting,
Black bats will be swooping when the sun is gone,
      That is all.

The spirit children are beneath,
They are all moving back and forth,
They roll in play among tufts of white eagle down,
      That is all.

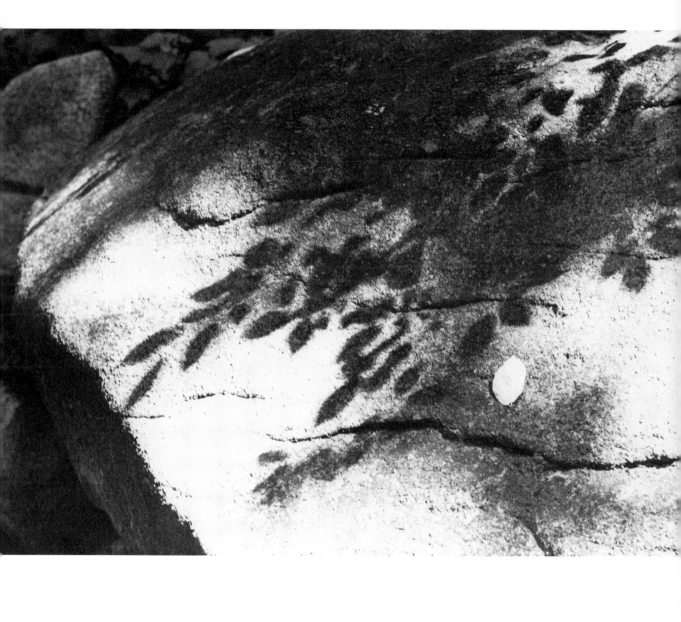

Fire-Fly Song

Flitting white-fire insects!
Wandering small-fire beasts!
Wave little stars about my bed!
Weave little stars into my sleep!
Come, little dancing white-fire bug,
Come, little flitting white-fire beast!
Light me with your white-flame magic,
Your little star-torch.

Song of the Crow and Owl

At midnight
      may I roam
      against the winds.
May I roam
      at night.
May I roam
      when the owl
      is hooting—
      may I roam.

At dawn
      may I roam
      against the winds.
May I roam
      at dawn.
May I roam
      when the crow
      is calling—
      may I roam.

We Are Singing in the Night

Now as the night is over us we are singing the songs
        that were given to us.
You see the clouds beginning to form on top of the mountains.
They look like little white feathers.
You will see them shake like feathers in the wind.
Soon the raindrops will fall and make our country beautiful.

In the Night

In the night
The rain comes down.
Yonder at the edge of the earth
There is a sound like cracking,
There is a sound like falling.
Down yonder it goes on slowly rumbling.
It goes on shaking.

life

Let Me See

Let me see, if this be real,
Let me see, if this be real,
Let me see, if this be real,
This life I am living?
You, Gods, who possess the skies
Let me see, if this is real,
This life I am living.

It Was the Wind

It was the wind that gave them life.
It is the wind that comes out of our mouths now that
       gives us life.
When this ceases to blow we die.
In the skin at the tips of our fingers we see the trail
       of the wind;
It shows us where the wind blew when our ancestors
       were created.

I Am Walking

Toward calm and shady places
I am walking
on the earth.

Be Still

Put your feet down with pollen*
Put your hands down with pollen.
Put your head down with pollen.
Then your feet are pollen;
Your hands are pollen;
Your body is pollen;
Your mind is pollen;
Your voice is pollen.
The trail is beautiful.
Be still.

* The pollen referred to in the song is a sacred ingredient
in many Navajo rituals symbolizing peace.

Song of the Butterfly

In the coming heat
    of the day
    I stood there.

This Song Cheers Me

For a long time I have been walking and seeing nothing;
Now I find this song and it cheers me.

Sing Your Song

Sing your song
Looking up at the sky.

My Music

My music
    reaches
    to the sky.

Friendly Song

The sky
Loves to hear me.

The Wind

Sometimes
I go about pitying myself
While I am carried by
The wind
Across the sky.

A Wolf I Considered Myself

A wolf
I considered myself
But
The owls are hooting
And
I fear the night.

By Tsakak

It is only crying about myself
                    that comes to me in song.

Need I Be Afraid

I am simply on the earth,
Need I be afraid?

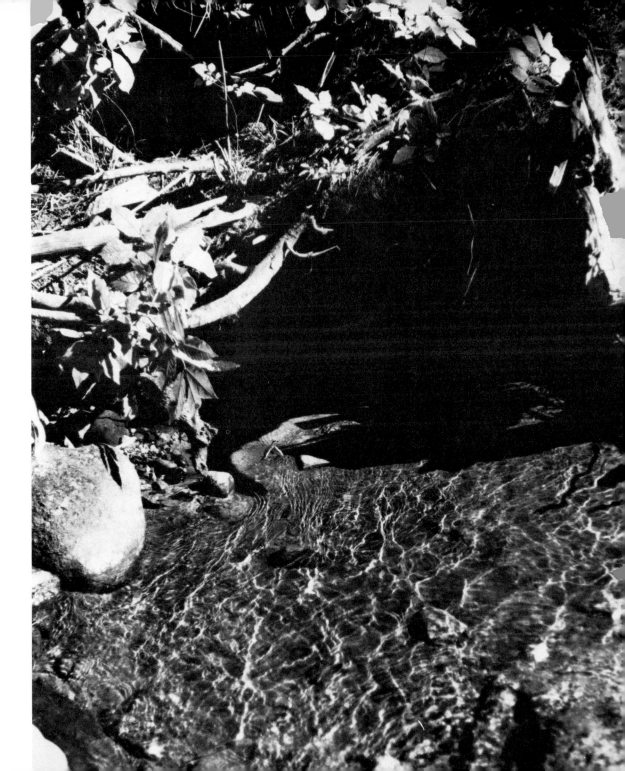

I Am Circling

I am circling like the vulture,
Staying, flying near the blue.
I am circling like the vulture
Breathing, flying near the blue.

As the Hawk Soars

Halfway up the sky
I am flying.

In the Flowers

I am standing in the flowers.
I am crawling in the flowers to my home.
In the midst of the bushes
On one branch
I am crawling up, I am crawling up.
I am standing in the flowers.
I am crawling in the flowers.

The Great Sea

The great sea
Has sent me adrift,
It moves me as the weed in a great river,
Earth and the great weather
Move me,
Have carried me away
And move my inward parts with joy.

That Wind

That wind, that wind,
Shakes my tipi, shakes my tipi,
And sings a song for me,
And sings a song for me.

Part of the Mountain Chant

In beauty may I walk.
All day long may I walk.
Through the returning seasons may I walk.
On the trail marked with pollen may I walk.
With grasshoppers about my feet may I
Walk.
With dew about my feet may I walk.
With beauty may I walk.
With beauty before me, may I walk.
With beauty behind me, may I walk.
With beauty below me, may I walk.
With beauty all around me, may I walk.
In old age wandering on a trail of beauty,
Lively, may I walk.
In old age, wandering on a trail of beauty,
Living again, may I walk.
It is finished in beauty.
It is finished in beauty.

love

Lullaby

Be still
Sleep.

Hopi Lullaby

Sleep, sleep, sleep.
In the trail, the beetles
On each other's backs are sleeping,
So on mine, my baby, you.
Sleep, sleep, sleep.

How Tiny You Are

Little baby, how tiny are you.

My Child

I made moccasins for him,
I made moccasins for him,
For I love him,
For I love him.

Soon I shall see my child,
Soon I shall see my child,
Says your mother,
Says your mother.

Come to Me Now

I am ready; come to me now, fearing nothing;
Come now to me here!
Little one,
Come, come to me here;
Fearing nothing, come!

The Child Is Introduced to the Cosmos at Birth

Ho! Ye Sun, Moon, Stars, all ye that
     move in the heavens,
  I bid you hear me!
Into your midst has come a new life.
     Consent ye, I implore!
Make its path smooth, that it may reach
     the brow of the first hill!

Ho! Ye Winds, Clouds, Rain, Mist, all ye
     that move in the air,
  I bid you hear me!
Into your midst has come a new life.
    Consent ye, I implore!

Make its path smooth, that it may reach
     the brow of the second hill!
Ho! Ye Hills, Valleys, Rivers, Lakes,
     Trees, Grasses, all ye of the earth,
  I bid you hear me!
Into your midst has come a new life.
    Consent ye, I implore!

Make its path smooth, that it may reach
    the brow of the third hill!
Ho! Ye Birds, great and small, that fly
    in the air,
Ho! Ye Animals, great and small, that
    dwell in the forest,
Ho! Ye insects that creep among the
    grasses and burrow in the ground—
    I bid you hear me!
Into your midst has come a new life.
    Consent ye, I implore!
Make its path smooth, that it may reach the
    brow of the fourth hill!

Ho! All ye of the heavens, all ye of the
    air, all ye of the earth:
    I bid you all to hear me!
Into your midst has come a new life.
    Consent ye, consent ye all, I implore!
Make its path smooth—then shall it travel
    beyond the four hills!

I Wish I Were a Cloud

I wish I were a cloud
So I could stay always in the air
And see him
All the time.

Love Song

No matter how hard I try
To forget you,
You always
Come back to my mind,
And when you hear me singing
You may know
I am weeping for you.

Around the Sky

Around the sky
I come to you with my sound.

Love Song

A loon I thought it was
But it was
My love's
Splashing oar.

You and I Shall Go

It is above that you and I shall go;
Along the Milky Way you and I shall go;
Along the flower trail you and I shall go;
Picking flowers on our way you and I shall go.

death

The Death Song of White Antelope

Nothing lives long
Nothing lives long
Nothing lives long
Except the earth and the mountains.

They Will Take Me Home

They will take me home
The spirits,
The thunders and wind,
They will take me home.

In This World

Oh! I have seen many things in this world,
I have been in this world a long time.

Song to the Raven

Raven
    I am going to die—
    fly away.

War Song

I cast it away,
My body.

Death Song of Namebines

The odor of death
I discern the odor of death
In the front of my body.

By Cgwatc

I always think within myself
       that there is no place
       where people do not die.

Concerning Wisdom, A Fragment

I perform the Beauty Way.
I am over eighty years old.
I have been learning since I was eleven years old.
I want someone to learn what I have been learning.

Death Song

In the great night my heart will go out.
Toward me the darkness comes rattling,
In the great night my heart will go out.

cosmos

Beseeching the Breath

Beseeching the breath of the divine one,
His life-giving breath,
His breath of old age,
His breath of waters,
His breath of seeds,
His breath of riches,
His breath of fecundity,
His breath of power
His breath of all good fortune,
Asking for his breath
And into my warm body drawing his breath,
I add to your breath
That happily you may always live.

When Our Earth Mother

When our earth mother is replete with living waters,
When spring comes,
The source of our flesh,
All the different kinds of corn,
We shall lay to rest in the ground.
With their earth mother's living waters,
They will be made into new beings.
Coming out standing into the daylight
Of their sun father,
Calling for rain,
To all sides they will stretch out their hands.
Then from wherever the rain makers stay quietly
They will send forth their misty breath;
Their massed clouds filled with water will come out
        and sit with us,
Far from their homes,
With outstretched hands of water they will embrace
        the corn,
Stepping down to caress them with their fresh waters,
With their fine rain caressing the earth,
And yonder, wherever the roads of the rain makers
        come forth,
Torrents will rush forth,
Silt will rush forth,

Mountains will be washed out,
Logs will be washed down,
Yonder all the mossy mountains will drip with water.
The clay-lined hollows of our earth mother
Will overflow with water,
Desiring that it should be thus,
I send forth my prayer.

Oft in My Travels

Often in my travels I come to the land of spirits,
As day approaches I travel and come to the land of spirits.

Often in my travels I come to the land of spirits,
As the sun drops, I travel and come to the land of spirits.

Often in my travels I come to the land of spirits,
In my dreams I travel and come to the land of spirits.

Often in my travels I come to the land of spirits,
As a spirit I travel and come to the land of spirits.

The Mystic Path

My footprints are even now upon the mystic path,
The spirit path that ever lies before us,
Truly, my footprints are on that path.
My footprints are even now upon that mystic path.

Cure Song

The evening glow yet lingers;
The evening glow yet lingers,
And I sit with my gourd rattle
Engaged in the sacred chant.
As I wave the eagle feathers
We hear the magic sounding.

Song of the Sky Loom*

O our Mother the Earth, O our Father the Sky,
Your children are we, and with tired backs
We bring you the gifts that you love.
Then weave for us a garment of brightness;
May the warp be the white light of morning,
May the weft be the red light of evening,
May the fringes be the falling rain,
May the border be the standing rainbow.
Thus weave for us a garment of brightness
That we may walk fittingly where birds sing,
That we may walk fittingly where the grass is green,
O our Mother the Earth, O our Father the Sky.

* "Sky loom" refers to isolated desert showers that hang, like clusters of threads, from the clouds.

Song of the Earth

All is beautiful,
All is beautiful,
All is beautiful, indeed.

Now the Mother Earth
And the Father Sky,
Meeting, joining one another,
Helpmates ever, they.
All is beautiful,
All is beautiful,
All is beautiful, indeed.

Warrior Song

I shall vanish and be no more,
But the land over which I now roam
Shall remain
And change not.

Wailing Song

The sky will weep,
The sky,
At the end of the earth;
The sky will weep.

Ghost Dance

We shall live again.
We shall live again.

Earth (**Always Endures**)

Earth
　　always
　　endures.

the songs

the origins of american indian songs and chants

The songs and chants of the American Indian were a totally integral part of tribal communication and life. While the use and significance of song forms differed from tribe to tribe and reflected varying levels of tribal development and culture, they were used as a regular part of daily life by all the North American civilizations.

Songs were magic. Some were so personal they could only be sung alone by the individual to whom the song had been given, usually in a vision or dream. These were often known simply as dream songs. A few outstanding examples can be found on pages 4, 25, 60, 64, 80 and 88. In most cases the individual's dream song was learned during a fasting ritual marking the transition from youth to manhood. Such songs were never "composed." Rather they came into the mind of the Indian when he placed himself in a receptive attitude. As the outstanding translator of Indian songs, Frances Densmore, describes in one of her many Bureau of American Ethnology reports:

> The Indian waited and listened for the mysterious
> power pervading all nature to speak to him in song.
> The Indian realized that he was part of nature—
> not akin to it. *BAE Bulletin* 151, P. 219.

Each song was so personal, similar in some ways to the eastern concept of a "mantra," that no other individual could sing it without the owner's permission. Occasionally the owner bestowed the song upon a friend or bequeathed it to the tribe on his death, but in many instances he died without having sung it to anyone but himself.

Love songs were often magic too. They rarely described an existing state of affairs (exceptions can be found on pages 72, 79 and 82) but rather were prayerlike descriptions of a desired event or emotion. The songs on pages 75, 76, 78 and 83 are examples of this form.

The "projected state" or "charm" song was by no means limited to love. It applied equally to "curing" songs performed as part of a healing ceremony (page 33), to songs of courage and bravery (87, 88, 93 and 99) to charms used to lure unsuspecting animals or enemy warriors and, perhaps best known of all, to the great ritual prayers for fertility, rain, abundant harvests and victory against the forces of danger.

These rituals formed the backbone of the tribal body—linking the needs and desires of the tribe to a recognition of the insignificance of man against the great powers of nature and gods. The Navajos were particularly known for the duration and complexity of their rituals many of which contained literally hundreds of songs and chants performed over five-to-nine-day periods. Pages 16, 18, 20, 44, 47 and 67 provide examples of Navajo rituals and pages 7, 14, 21, 103 and 104 are extracts from rituals of the Hopi and Zuni tribes.

Compared to many of the other songs, the rituals were highly formal sequences of prayers requiring remarkable memory power by the participants. The omission of one line or even one word from any one of the hundreds of songs in a ritual, could lead to its immediate abandonment. Yet only in exceptional cases, such as the Zuni Creation Cycle or some of the Chippewa rituals, were the songs actually recorded in ideograph form, usually on birch bark.

Although words were considered sacred because of their strong magic powers, the impact of these songs came not from the words themselves but from the total integration of words, meaning, melody, rhythm, and movement. One could not be separated from the others. The concept of "lyrics" as opposed to "music" was nonexistent. The song was the whole. The song was the effect on the mind not the ears. The song was the power to control and to change.

While the selections contained in the book reflect the range and beauty of these songs, they can regrettably give little indication of their meaning and importance to the tribes from which they came. Take the simple

> We shall live again
> We shall live again   p. 115

Whole cycles of tribal experience lie behind such clean and absolute phrasing. In this instance, the stanza is part of the famous ghost dance—a combined expression by many Indian tribes during the late nineteenth century of their opposition to the tyranny of the white settlers, their belief in tribal restoration and in the ultimate annihilation of the intruders. The ghost dance was a prayer for renaissance—a rebirth of the great Indian culture on the North American continent.

In a less dramatic mood, the same economy of language can be seen in:

> I am simply on the earth,
> Need I be afraid?   p. 58

The Indian also possessed the ability to identify totally with living creatures—to see events through the eyes of a mouse, an eagle, a deer. Again while these songs had distinct magical properties, today their appeal lies in the words and clarity of perception (see pages 11, 37, 48 and 62).

The Indian used few qualifying adjectives in his songs; he sketched the thought, and the poetic temperament of his hearers supplied the gradations of color. The Indian often expressed himself in silence. Next to silence came the short song, with its rhythmic form, its simplicity and delicacy of expression. The songs on pages 2, 26, 27, 30, 114, 115, 116 are examples of the purest poetic descriptions. This one is particularly beautiful:

> The water bug is drawing the shadows of evening toward him
> Across the water.   p. 30

The translator, Ruth Underhill, once asked why most of the songs consisted only of a few lines. Her Indian informant replied: "The song is so short because we know so much."

It is this knowledge that makes the songs so powerful even today. Running through the dream songs, the love songs, the charms, the rituals, and the prayer songs is a total awareness of the unity and harmony of all things, animate and inanimate, physical and spiritual. Man is seen as being completely integrated with the forces of nature. Man is a vehicle through which the energies of the universe pass and are intensified. Take the song

> They will take me home
> The spirits,
> The thunders and wind,
> They will take me home   p. 88

Could there be a clearer statement of man's relationship to himself and the forces of life and energy that surround him?

And yet at the same time, there are those songs that express human frailties—inadequacies in the face of overwhelming powers:

> A wolf
> I considered myself
> But
> The owls are hooting
> And
> I fear the night   p. 55

Thus the Indian, while aware of his relationship to the cosmos, never completely lost that consciousness of himself as an independent entity (see pages 54, 55, 56, 65, 90, 94 and 96).

It is perhaps this characteristic that makes the Indian so recognizable. He was neither "noble" nor "savage." He was a human struggling to overcome the pettiness of the human condition and attain a closer association with the forces and energies that surrounded him. His songs are as full of meaning and as relevant today as they were when originally sung—centuries ago.

the translations

Most of the selections contained in this book are original translations published in the U. S. Bureau of American Ethnology bulletins and reports between 1888 and 1963. The translators, each carefully chosen by the BAE as an expert in American Indian history and the culture of one or more individual tribes, include: Ruth Bunzel, Frances Densmore, Alice Fletcher, Francis LaFlésche, Washington Matthews, Frank Russell, and J. R. Swanton.

Selections have also been made from publications by Natalie Curtis, Robert Lowie, Knud Rasmussen, Herbert J. Spinden, George Bird Grinnell, Ruth Underhill, Henry R. Schoolcraft, and Harriet Converse.

References are structured as follows:

> TRIBE/Translator
> Title of source. Author
> Publisher. Date of Publication. Page reference.
>
> General comments on the origins or meaning of the song.
>
> *In the case of all BAE publications, the translator is the author.*

page 2 TETON SIOUX/Frances Densmore
BAE Bulletin 61, 1918. P. 300.

page 4 PAPAGO/Frances Densmore
BAE Bulletin 90, 1929. P. 129.

page 5 PAPAGO/Frances Densmore
BAE Bulletin 90, 1929. P. 133.

page 6 PAPAGO/Ruth Underhill
Singing for Power: The Song Magic of the Papago Indians of Southern Arizona, Ruth Underhill.
University of California Press, 1938. P. 140.

page 7 HOPI/H. R. Voth
Field Museum of Natural History Anthropological Publications,
Vol. 6. No. I. 1903. P. 26.

The Oraibi Oáqöl ceremony of the Hopi Indians was one of a number of long ceremonies recorded by Reverend H. R. Voth. It is conducted by the tribe usually in October or November and is primarily a series of prayers for health and fertility. This song is normally sung in the early morning of the fifth day. (Also see p. 33.)

page 9 PAWNEE/Alice Fletcher
BAE Twenty-second Annual Report, 1900–1. P. 324.

The Hako is a major Pawnee ceremony. In essence, it is a prayer for children, a plea for tribal fertility strength, long life, happiness and peace.
    Alice Fletcher recorded the ceremony in 1898 and explains its form and significance: "Its fundamental ideas and teachings which are among the most important for the welfare of the people, are steadily unfolded from the initial rite to the final act through a long series of observances which are replete with detail and accompanied by nearly one hundred songs."
    These brief extracts from the long ceremony are from Alice Fletcher's original translation. (See also page 34.)

page 10 NOOTKA/Frances Densmore
BAE Bulletin 124, 1939. P. 285.

See "Sing Your Song" (p. 51) and its note.

page 11 PAPAGO/Ruth Underhill
Singing for Power: The Song Magic of the Papago Indians of Southern Arizona, Ruth Underhill.
University of California Press, 1938. P. 52.

page 12 YAQUI/R. Wilder
BAE Bulletin 186, 1963. P. 194.

page 13 PAPAGO/Frances Densmore
BAE Bulletin 90, 1929. P. 173.

This simple song, sung on salt-collecting expeditions by the Papago, reflects an understanding of the relationships between sea, wind, clouds, and rain.

page 14 ZUNI/M. C. Stevenson
BAE Twenty-third Annual Report, 1904. P. 176.

page 16 NAVAJO/Natalie Curtis
The Indian's Book: Songs and Legends of the American Indians, Natalie Curtis.
Dover, 1968. P. 365.

page 18 NAVAJO/Washington Matthews
"Songs of Sequence," Washington Matthews, *Journal of American Folk Lore,*
Vol. VII. P. 191.

This song is one of the forty songs of the House God which are normally sung as part of the Night-Chant ceremony—a major Navajo ritual of many days' duration.

page 20 NAVAJO/Washington Matthews
BAE Fifth Annual Report, 1888–89. P. 459.

The song is from the nine-day mountain chant ceremony, one of a large number of such ceremonies practiced by the Shamans, or medicine men, of the Navajo tribe. Like other great rites, it has its secret ceremonies but, unlike the others, ends with a varied celebration in the open air.

The primary purpose of the ceremony is to cure disease, but it is also the occasion for invoking the unseen powers on behalf of all tribal members especially for good crops and abundant rains.

page 21 HOPI/Natalie Curtis
The Indian's Book: Songs and Legends of the American Indians, Natalie Curtis.
Dover, 1968. Pp. 484–85.

The use of the "dualism" form and the colors of yellow and blue representing male and female is a familiar characteristic of fertility-directed rituals.

page 22 PAIUTE/James Mooney
BAE Fourteenth Annual Report, 1892–93. Pp. 1,054–55.

These and many other songs formed part of the Ghost Dance religion, a belief in a renewal of the earth and the elimination of all foreign oppressors. The religion was widespread among the Sioux, Paiute, Omaha, Cheyenne, Arapaho, and Winnebago tribes during the late nineteenth century. Although the Ghost Dance was only one of a long series of Indian rituals it was made particularly powerful by the presence of a messiah. The massacre at Wounded Knee effectively terminated the religious impact.

page 23 ACOMA/Frances Densmore
BAE Bulletin 165, 1957. P. 38.

In February or March the Acoma Indians hold a dance "as an invitation to the flowers to bloom again." The dance is accompanied by a series of evocative songs such as this delightful image of a butterfly.

page 25 WINTUN/D. Demetracopoulou
"Wintun Songs," D. Demetracopoulou, in *Anthropos*
Vol. 30, 1935. P. 485.

The "Northern Wintun" culture was particularly evident in northern California and the Upper Sacramento Valley. Its folklore was rich in legends and myths, many of which found an enthusiastic audience among East Coast residents following a series of articles in the New York *Sun* during the 1890s. Their beautiful songs full of fine images, are less well known. (See pages 78 and 83.)

page 26 CHIPPEWA/Frances Densmore
BAE Bulletin 45, 1910. P. 41.

page 27 CHIPPEWA/Frances Densmore
BAE Bulletin 53, 1913. P. 254.

page 28 OMAHA/Alice Fletcher and Francis LaFlésche
BAE Twenty-seventh Annual Report, 1905–6. P. 572.

This is part of the ritual of the primal rock. It reveals how closely the Indian identified with and respected the almost human presence of nature.

page 30 YAQUI/Frances Densmore
BAE Bulletin 110, 1932. P. 132.

page 31 PAPAGO/Ruth Underhill
Singing for Power: The Song Magic of the Papago Indians of Southern Arizona, Ruth Underhill.
University of California Press, 1938. P. 44.

page 32 YUMA/Frances Densmore
BAE Bulletin 110, 1932. P. 139.

This is a combination of two short songs, both part of the Yuma tribe Deer Dance that celebrates the mysterious powers of the deer.

page 33 PAPAGO/Frances Densmore
BAE Bulletin 90, 1929. P. 117.

This Papago song relates to the treatment of the sick and is said to have been received, for this purpose, from spirits of the dead. The song "belongs" to the Owl-woman, a revered Papago medicine-woman. (See also page 99.)

page 34 PAPAGO/Frances Densmore
BAE Bulletin 90, 1929. Pp. 113–14.

page 36 OJIBWA/Henry R. Schoolcraft
Onéota or the Characteristics of the Red Race of America, H. R. Schoolcraft
Wiley and Putnam, New York, 1845. P. 347.

page 37 TETON SIOUX/Frances Densmore
BAE Bulletin 61, 1918. P. 186.

page 38 PAPAGO/Frances Densmore
BAE Bulletin 90, 1929. P. 142.

page 39 PAPAGO/Ruth Underhill
Singing for Power: The Song Magic of the Papago Indians of Southern Arizona, Ruth Underhill.
University of California Press, 1938. P. 154.

page 43 PAWNEE/H. J. Spinden
Songs of the Tewa, Herbert J. Spinden
Exposition of Indian Tribal Arts. New York, 1933. P. 13.

Spinden describes this as a war song with an unusual metaphysical turn. It is sung when a warrior ventures out to a war from which it is likely he will never return.

page 44 NAVAJO/Washington Matthews
Navajo Legends, Washington Matthews.
Houghton Mifflin Company, 1897. P. 69.

This song is taken from Part I of the legend of Navajo origins, which has four distinct parts:
1. The story of emergence
2. Early events in the fifth world
3. The war gods
4. The growth of the Navajo nation

page 46 CHIPPEWA/Frances Densmore
BAE Bulletin 45, 1910. P. 110.

page 47 NAVAJO/Washington Matthews
Navajo Legends, Washington Matthews.
Houghton Mifflin Company, 1897. P. 109.

See "It Was the Wind" (p. 44) and its note. This song is taken from part three of the Navajo legend.

page 48 CHIPPEWA/Frances Densmore
BAE Bulletin 53, 1913. P. 179.

page 50 Indians of British Columbia/Frances Densmore
BAE Bulletin 136, 1943. P. 36.

page 51 NOOTKA/Frances Densmore
BAE Bulletin 124, 1939. P. 276.

The Nootka (Makah and Clayoquot) and Quileute tribes were scattered around the Vancouver island area and the northern sector of the Washington coast. (See also pages 73 and 79.)

page 52 CHIPPEWA/Frances Densmore
BAE Bulletin 45, 1910. P. 163.

page 53 CHIPPEWA/Frances Densmore
BAE Bulletin 45, 1910. P. 209.

page 54 CHIPPEWA/Frances Densmore
BAE Bulletin 45, 1910. P. 127.

page 55 TETON SIOUX/Frances Densmore
BAE Bulletin 61, 1918. P. 339.

page 56 TLINGIT/John Swanton
BAE Bulletin 39, 1909. P. 401.

page 58 MANDAN/Frances Densmore
BAE Bulletin 80, 1923. P. 121.

page 60 PIMA/Frank Russell
BAE Twenty-sixth Annual Report, 1904–5. P. 295.

page 61 CHIPPEWA/Frances Densmore
BAE Bulletin 45, 1910. P. 131.

page 62 YAQUI/R. Wilder
BAE Bulletin 186, 1963. P. 195.

page 64 ESKIMO/Knud Rasmussen
(retranslated from the Danish by W. J. Worster). Originally in
Intellectual Culture of the Iglulik Eskimos, Knud Rasmussen.
Copenhagen, 1929.

page 65 KIOWA/ James Mooney
BAE Fourteenth Annual Report, 1892–93. P. 1,087.

page 67 NAVAJO/Washington Matthews
Navajo Myths, Prayers and Songs.
University of California Press, 1907. Pp. 48–49.

See "Twelfth Song of the Thunder" (p. 20) and its note.

page 70 TETON SIOUX/Frances Densmore
BAE Bulletin 61, 1918. P. 493.

page 72 HOPI/Natalie Curtis
The Indian's Book: Songs and Legends of the American Indians, Natalie Curtis.
Dover, 1968. P. 480.

This lullaby is one of the oldest Hopi songs. It is still sung in many Hopi villages and there is perhaps scarcely a Hopi who has not been lulled to sleep with its refrain of "pura, pura, pura" (sleep, sleep, sleep).

page 73 NOOTKA/Frances Densmore
BAE Bulletin 124, 1939. P. 217.

page 74 SIOUX/James Mooney
BAE Fourteenth Annual Report, 1892–93. Pp. 1,074–75.

page 75 PAWNEE/Alice Fletcher
BAE Twenty-second Annual Report, 1900–1. P. 349.

"Come to Me Now," part of the Pawnee Hako ceremony (see p. 9) is addressed to the child, who, surrounded by creative forces, is urged to move, to arise, as this song is sung.

page 76 OMAHA/Alice Fletcher
BAE Twenty-seventh Annual Report, 1905–6. Pp. 115–16.

When an Omaha child was born it was not regarded as a member of the tribe but simply as a living being entering the universe, whose coming must be ceremonially announced in order to assure it an accepted place in the living world. This announcement reflected the Omaha belief in the oneness of the universe through the bond of "life-power" that pervaded all things in nature, animate and inanimate.

The four "hills" referred to in the song mark the stages of life: infancy, youth, manhood, and old age.

page 78 Indians of British Columbia/Frances Densmore
BAE Bulletin 136, 1943. P. 81.

page 79 NOOTKA/Frances Densmore
BAE Bulletin 124, 1939. P. 327.

See "Sing Your Song" (p. 51) and its note.

page 80 CHIPPEWA/Frances Densmore
BAE Bulletin 53, 1913. P. 274.

page 82 CHIPPEWA/Frances Densmore
BAE Bulletin 45, 1910. P. 150.

page 83 WINTUN/D. Demetracopoulou
"Wintun Songs," D. Demetracopoulou, in *Anthropos*
Vol. 30, 1935, P. 485.

See "Dream Song" (p. 25) and its note.

page 87 CHEYENNE/George Bird Grinnell
The Fighting Cheyenne.
Charles Scribner's Sons, New York, 1915. P. 171.

These words were sung by White Antelope, a Cheyenne, just before he was shot down by
the U. S. Cavalry during the Sand Creek Massacre of November 1864, during which more
than six hundred Indians were killed without warning.

page 88 CHIPPEWA/Frances Densmore
*BAE Bulleti*n 45, 1910. P. 198.

page 90 PAPAGO/Frances Densmore
BAE Bulletin 90, 1929. P. 28.

page 92 MANDAN/Frances Densmore
BAE Bulletin 80, 1923. P. 49.

page 93 OJIBWA/Henry R. Schoolcraft
Onéota or the Characteristics of the Red Race of America
Wiley and Putnam, New York, 1845. P. 347.

Henry Schoolcraft, assisted by a young Chippewa warrior, recorded a series of war songs
by the Ojibwa Algonquins during one of his many many expeditions to remote parts of
America. This particular song is an expression of great courage, an attitude of sacrifice and
bravery prior to battle.

page 94 CHIPPEWA/Frances Densmore
BAE Bulletin 53, 1913. P. 114.

page 95 TLINGIT/John R. Swanton
BAE Bulletin 39, 1909. P. 410.

page 96 NAVAJO/From *Rouch Rock News,* Chinle, Arizona, September 24, 1969.

The "beauty way" is a Navajo curing chant, a major ceremony.

page 99 PAPAGO/Frances Densmore
BAE Bulletin 90, 1929. P. 126.

See "Brown Owls" (p. 33) and its note.

page 103 ZUNI/Ruth Bunzel
BAE Forty-seventh Annual Report, 1929–30. P. 701 (two lines omitted).

The preliminary initiation of Zuni children takes place every fourth year. Prior to the ceremony itself a long chant is intoned describing the mythological implications of the ceremony. This is the final segment of that chant.

page 104 ZUNI/Ruth Bunzel
BAE Forty-seventh Annual Report, 1929–30. P. 484.

Zuni prayers were highly structured and articulate sequences of requests. The sophistication of this particular culture is evident from Ruth Bunzel's translation; yet the requests are direct and pragmatic as in this prayer for rain.

page 107 OSAGE /Francis LaFlésche
BAE Forty-fifth Annual Report, 1927–28. P. 597.

A belief in a future spiritual state of existence is strong among the Osage people, and this song expresses the proximity of the spiritual state of being to the singer's human existence. The same feeling is expressed even more directly in the following song (p. 108).

page 108 OSAGE/Francis LaFlésche
BAE Forty-fifth Annual Report, 1927–28. P. 598.

page 109 PIMA/Frank Russell
BAE Twenty-sixth Annual Report, 1904–5. P. 302.

This song was sung by a Blackwater medicine man when making his diagnosis of a case.

page 110 TEWA/Herbert J. Spinden
Songs of the Tewa, Herbert J. Spinden
Exposition of Indian Tribal Arts, New York, 1933. P. 94.

page 111 NAVAJO/Natalie Curtis
The Indian's Book: Songs and Legends of the American Indians, Natalie Curtis.
Dover, 1968. P. 372.

An almost perfect expression of the Navajo concept of unity among all natural forces and the totally complementary nature of contrasting elements, this is a benediction on the world.

page 112 OMAHA/Alice Fletcher and Francis LaFlésche
BAE Twenty-seventh Annual Report, 1904–6. P. 431.

page 114 FOX/Truman Michelson
BAE Bulletin 72, 1921. P. 29.

page 115 COMANCHE/James Mooney
BAE Fourteenth Annual Report, 1892. P. 1,047.

page 116 MANDAN/Frances Densmore
BAE Bulletin 80, 1923. P. 50.